NELL HILL'S
rooms we love

NELL HILL'S
rooms
we
love

Mary Carol Garrity

Photography by Bob Greenspan

**Andrews McMeel
Publishing, LLC**

Kansas City • Sydney • London

Andrews McMeel Publishing, LLC
an Andrews McMeel Universal Company
1130 Walnut Street, Kansas City, Missouri 64106

www.andrewsmcmeel.com

13 14 15 16 17 WKT 10 9 8 7 6 5 4 3 2 1

ISBN: 978-1-4494-2164-9

Library of Congress Control Number: 2013933507

Book Design by Diane Marsh
Cover Design by Julie Barnes
Book Developed by Jean Lowe, River House Media, Inc., Leawood, Kansas
Photograph p. 114-115 © 2012 Earl Richardson

Attention: Schools and Businesses
Andrews McMeel books are available at quantity discounts with
bulk purchase for educational, business, or sales promotional use.
For information, please e-mail the Andrews McMeel Publishing
Special Sales Department: specialsales@amuniversal.com

To the Global Orphan Project

contents

introduction

VERY YEAR AT my Nell Hill's stores, the staff and I consult
with thousands of customers who come to visit us, seeking
advice and inspiration. Projects can range from finding the perfect pillow for
their sofa to the mirror in the entryway to whole house makeovers. No job is too
small or too large for us—all design challenges energize us. The ultimate goal,
no matter the size of the project, is to help our customers add sparkle or sizzle
to their homes.

My personal passion is to work with homeowners to make the rooms in
their houses beautiful, colorful, functional, and special. In *Nell Hill's Rooms We
Love*, I hope to share some of my favorite rooms—rooms we all fell in love with
during the process of offering our decorating solutions. These are rooms that
truly reflect the goals of our customers—it is our honor to work with them and
watch their dreams come to life.

If it is a big project, like a whole room makeover or even a whole house design,
we can help customers decide everything from the rugs for the floor to the trim on
the drapery panels. It is a big challenge to think about redoing a room in a house—
committing to a paint color or wallpaper, dozens of yards of fabric, new upholstery,
area rugs that you will be living with awhile, and then there's also the investment
of dollars and time spent on the makeover. In these pages, I hope to demystify the
process by showing you through rooms that we think capture the spirit of Nell Hill's
while calling out details that go into making the room successful.

To me, success in decorating means that I succeed in helping customers
identify their own personal style. While my stores are packed full of room
settings, tableaus, and both big and little surprises, I believe that people have

a personal style that is uniquely their own. Our goal at Nell Hill's is to help you discover your style by offering some simple guidelines for your decisions.

Even though it has been more than ten years since I published my first book, I think you will see that there are certain guiding principles at work here that still inform my advice on design. At Nell Hill's

- We believe that your style comes from mixing old with new, showcasing your keepsake treasures as well as your newly discovered surprises. I often remind customers to remember that your home is not your "mother's house," but your mother's keepsakes can be beautifully accented in new ways.

- We believe in comfort—cozy, inviting rooms that provide spaces where you can sit down with a book or get comfortable with your guests, who should always find a special amenity waiting just for them.

- We believe that a beautiful room always offers an unexpected delight.

- We believe that you should try to bring the outdoors inside, using garden structures year-round in seasonal decorating.

In this book, my staff and I will apply Nell Hill's principles of design to all-new challenges. Even though design styles and trends have changed significantly since my first book (*Style at Home*) ten years ago, we will rediscover those same principles at work in four very different houses. In the following pages, we will visit rooms inspired by the needs of each of the four homeowners and will see how they transformed their rooms using Nell Hill's inspiration and tricks of the trade. We will study

- A century-old English Tudor in a city neighborhood—reinvented by Marsee and Mike Bates, who are now empty nesters

- A suburban teardown—redesigned for Anne and Andy Epstein's growing family

- The traditional country home of Julie and Marc Wenger that was rebuilt because of structural problems but retains its old soul.

- A sweeping country manor—built by Beth and Mike Fox, with one-of-a kind rooms

Finally, we will revisit my home, where I will update you on changes that I have made that are influenced by trends and color.

While traveling through the pages of these homes, we will reconstruct the process and provide readers with the blueprint to use for discovering your own personal styles. You will see that the function of the room, color trends, fabrics, accessories, and whimsical touches help inform decorating decisions.

At the back of the book, you will also see the style boards—choices that set the mood for the project—that we developed with each homeowner. In this Design Portfolio that starts on page 102, you will see the home reassembled with the homeowners' fabrics, paint colors, and the patterns that informed their decisions.

Chapter by chapter, we will tour stylish rooms from different homes and I will point out what elements went into the design of each room. I will share with you what informed the design decisions that each homeowner made. We hope you will be inspired by these rooms—like I am—and will come away with creative energy to make your rooms beautiful, functional, colorful, and comfortable.

Fondly,

Mary Carol Garrity

functional and fabulous

ORE THAN EVER before, people are entertaining at home, and in this chapter I would love to show you through rooms that make great use of space. The concept of a living room that is off-limits to the rest of the family is no longer viable, and people are learning to live larger in smaller spaces. Or in larger spaces with oversized rooms, we are breaking down the functionality of the room into multiple-use areas.

Organization is so important with the addition of mudrooms and larger laundry areas. Bathrooms are now home spas where all of the toiletries and accessories needed for relaxation are close at hand. Well-organized rooms can be beautiful and functional, as you will find out in this chapter.

Empty nesters are turning bedrooms into home offices. And guest rooms are equipped with all the amenities for when your children and friends do come for a visit. Playrooms—for grown-ups and little ones—can coexist with style and whimsy.

Or if your family is in a growth spurt, why not consider that the design of the room can grow with the children and can evolve with your kids over time.

Outdoor living is also a growing trend, and we now think of the green spaces outside our windows as part of our living space. More than ever, customers want to extend their living beyond the front and back doors. At Nell Hill's we are always looking for ways to bring the inside out, or the outside in. On my porch, I use furniture in much the same way I would indoors.

What defines your space? Perhaps a tour of these beautiful rooms, reinvented by you, will help you discover new purposes and reasons to stay home!

WHEN EMPTY NESTERS *Marsee and Mike relocated, they bought a traditional three-bedroom English Tudor in the heart of the city. They set about redefining how to use the classic floor plan of the home in new ways. They converted one of the bedrooms into Mike's home office, which includes this decidedly masculine leather chair and ottoman for reading and relaxing. The burled walnut bookcases are family heirlooms and wrap three walls of the room. The brown walls give the room warmth and allow the old-world crown molding and woodwork to define the room.*

WHEN JULIE AND MARC *Wegner were forced*
to rebuild their country dream home because
of foundation issues, Julie decided to seize the
opportunity to build the house of her dreams. One
of her priorities was to redesign the laundry room,
where she spent much of her time with a busy household of five. She chose a fabulous farmhouse-
style cupboard in which she could stylishly store linens below and serving ware above. Atop the
cabinet she showcases an heirloom quilt. The addition of a dramatic pink paint color on the ceiling
took the room to new heights. The café curtains let the morning light in, providing a sunny space
for her to go about her morning chores.

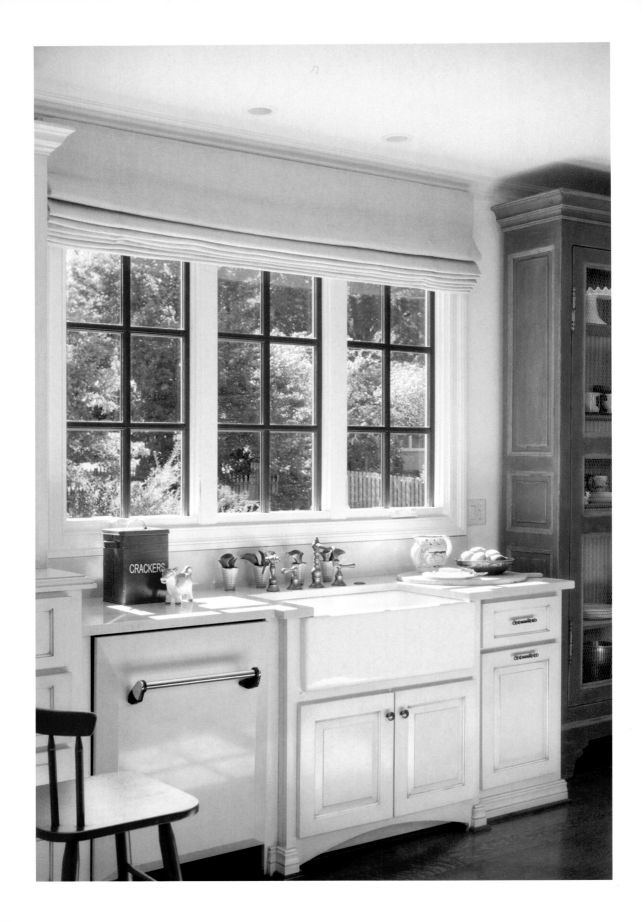

SEPARATING THE KITCHEN *sink from the main cooking area in her large new kitchen allowed Anne to open up more workspace throughout the room. The large farmhouse sink also afforded her a sunny spot that overlooked the yard, where she could see the children while washing the dishes.*

One of Anne and Andy Epstein's priorities when they tore down a house and rebuilt their dream home on the same site was to have plenty of organized space for their growing family of three young children. In the redesign, the house gained a side-entry mudroom where everyone could drop off personal belongings before entering the kitchen area.

A MAGAZINE ARTICLE that featured a black island detailed in gold with hand-forged metal scrollwork inspired Anne and Andy's kitchen. The kitchen they built and designed matched their dreams and exceeded their wishes in many ways. The AGA range adds a European flair to the room, along with the large metal advertising sign that visually separates the large kitchen space from the main living areas. The oversized sliding barn doors that separate the two rooms were reclaimed and serve many purposes—they add creative drama and functionality and divide the spaces into separate areas when needed.

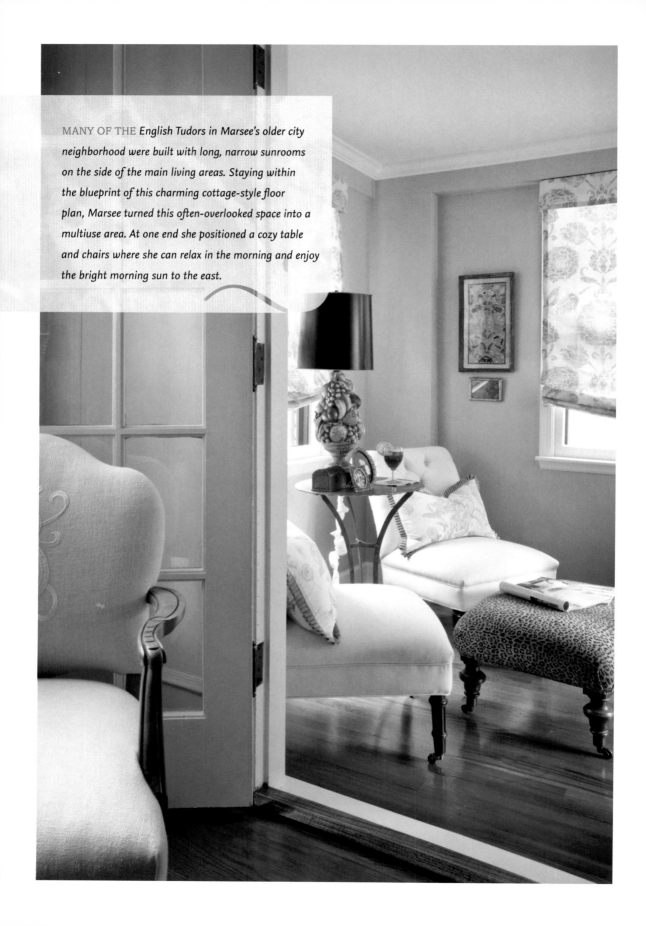

MANY OF THE *English Tudors in Marsee's older city neighborhood were built with long, narrow sunrooms on the side of the main living areas. Staying within the blueprint of this charming cottage-style floor plan, Marsee turned this often-overlooked space into a multiuse area. At one end she positioned a cozy table and chairs where she can relax in the morning and enjoy the bright morning sun to the east.*

MARSEE USED COOL *neutral tones of white throughout the entire home, which makes the space seem larger and more open. On the opposite end of the room she positioned a small bench with a basket underneath that conceals her computer modems and cables. A garden urn holds decorative glass balls, bringing the charm of the outdoors into this sunny room.*

Down the middle of the room, on the long wall, Marsee set up this stylish bar service. This long and narrow room now serves many purposes, and the addition of the service area guarantees that all of the square footage of this cozy Tudor will be utilized. Guests will be drawn now to this previously overlooked space.

fabulous and functional　9

AT THE FRONT *door of Julie's country home, the center-hall entry with its spacious hallway affords a view to the back of the house. This is where you get a straightaway view of the glossy black doors in the back hallway where Julie placed her own private retreat.*

JULIE NEEDED HER *own private space to relax, read, and watch her favorite television shows. When she redesigned her country home, she guaranteed herself this sanctuary and cozy retreat that overlooks the land at the back of the house. She, too, can enjoy the morning sun while leisurely paging through her favorite magazine. It's become a favorite spot for her husband, too, who enjoys the quiet and comfortable space for watching movies and the evening news together.*

IN SIMILAR FASHION, Anne envisioned a television room separate from the rest of the living areas. This stylish den that overlooks the front and wraps to the side of the home provides all of the amenities that she could want and the privacy that she craves with three active children in the house. The center-hall plan divides this private den from the formal dining room on the other side of the foyer and the great room and kitchen at the back of the house.

A MEDIA CONSOLE *conceals all of the wires and cables needed to run the electronics while keeping the room clean and stylish at the same time. The boldest color in the room comes from the pops of bright orange pottery on the console—shades of the same color are repeated in accents throughout the house.*

The chesterfield sofa is situated between two windows. The color palette is soft and soothing and the wall décor is understated in support of the quiet space. Matching architectural prints anchor the space above the sofa.

BETH AND MIKE *Fox built a grand manor home on 350 acres of coveted land that once was home to a girls' camp in the country. The grandeur of the stone home that sits high atop a hill can be seen for miles around. The scale of the home is captured in the multifunctional great room and dining area that sit side by side in the same room, attached to the large kitchen, just out of view.*

To furnish such a grand room and still create defined seating required two extra-long sofas (108 inches long) and an oversized ottoman. I especially like the way the two different sofa styles—a chesterfield rolled-arm and a high-back with split ridge sides—work so well together. The plaid wing chairs flank the fireplace, and a separate seating area is placed at the stairwell for quieter conversations.

The curved staircase can be seen from top to bottom on all three floors of the house. Windows of various shapes and sizes are positioned to provide panoramic views of this gorgeous property.

fabulous and functional   15

THE LANDING AT *the top of the stairs above the great room features a gorgeous billiard table that sits in an open game room. Through the glass doors, you can see Mike's office seating area with a fireplace on one end. Again, the use of artwork displayed in grids—here a set of pheasants—helps define the room. The compatible colors of the two area rugs add continuity to the décor.*

THE DINING TABLE *on one side of the great room was hand-hewn from wood that was harvested from the property, as are all of the wood floors and ceilings in the home. This table was built to seat their children and grandchildren—part of their large, growing, multigenerational family that gathers often at the new home built for entertaining.*

Outside the gorgeous arched porch doors you will see rockers that are set about the wraparound loggia, which offers spots for just sitting and enjoying the many vistas afforded by this special property.

MARSEE WASN'T CONTENT
to have her small kitchen breakfast
room relegated to a predictable
kitchen table and chairs. She
reinvented the small space, which
has the benefit of the northeast
corner at the back of the house, as
a comfortable and quaint place to share morning coffee and the newspaper.

This is not your ordinary kitchen sink. Situated directly across from the breakfast room
seating, the sink makes the chore of doing dishes a lot more enjoyable for Marsee. Look how she
stylishly disguised the cleaning utensils. They sit in a footed silver tray just below her little café-
curtained window overlooking the backyard.

fabulous and functional   19

"The spaces outside our doors and windows are more beautiful and functional than ever. A beautiful room doesn't need walls to hold it!"

ANNE AND ANDY *wanted their outdoor living to be as stylish and comfortable as their inside living. Just beyond the family room's doors of their rebuilt suburban home, they built a stone fireplace with seating all around. On this particular fall day, their new home was open on a homes tour. The black and white area rug anchors the area, where pops of orange color inside are carried outside for a celebration of autumn.*

color changes everything

HE EVOLUTION OF any beautiful room begins with the choice of color that we decide to use on the main surfaces. A dark color can make a room cozy, warm, and inviting. Colors inspired by nature—whether it is a sunny yellow or bright grass-green—help to connect the inside and outside of a home. Add a bold paint color to the ceiling and the mood of the room is instantly elevated.

When Julie turned her adult children loose creating guest rooms that they would love to visit, one of her daughters chose this stylish dresser. I love the way that this bold pop of turquoise is crowned with a gold starburst mirror. It is a great fresh and modern take on traditional furniture.

If I had to point to one major change in my decorating philosophy over the past ten years it would be the introduction of bold color accents into home décor.

In my own home, I have opted for neutrals on my walls and windows. Over the years, I have used many combinations of white fabrics in all shades of creamy white to define my living spaces, along with cream-colored shutters and trim on my large windows. I find whites soothing and restful, and the many shades of white when mixed together provide an interesting neutral palette to work with when introducing color. The interplay of whites and neutrals also allows me to experiment with bold color and seasonal accent colors, like orange in autumn and red in winter, without competing with other essential elements in the room.

Color is the first brushstroke that informs our decorating decisions. In the rooms in this chapter, you will find that traditional elements of any room can be reinvented with the use of bold color. The color can be on the walls, the floor, the ceiling, or even on a small pillow, but every beautiful room will showcase how color worked its magic on the space.

JULIE'S SOARING TWO-STORY *entry is bathed in sunny yellow. The entire house lets outdoor light in through the generous placement of divided-light windows everywhere.*

In her large open kitchen at the back of the entry, the bright grass-green complements the use of yellow seen here in the entry hall through the transom doorway. The use of botanicals and birds—featured in the oversized wall art as well as on the fabric slipcover—adds to the natural theme of the décor. Julie's bold choice to use architectural gray on her island—and shades of gray that appear throughout her home—sets this room apart and provides a unique focal point that holds its own in the bright space.

WHEN JULIE REDESIGNED her home, which sits on several acres and a sunny slope overlooking a lake, one of her first priorities was to have a large eat-in kitchen that could provide a gathering spot for her family and daily drop-in friends. Julie wanted to be part of the action while cooking, but the space needed to be large enough to accommodate everyone. She actually intended for it to function more as a second dining room.

*"Pillows talk:
One of the simplest
and most economical
ways to make color
statements is in the use
of accent pillows."*

I LOVE THE *way that Marsee's soothing whites of the
living room allow her to add color throughout the year
in the pillow accessories she chooses. The black screen
behind the all-white sofa gives the needed definition to
the seating area of the room and elegantly provides the
needed height and scale to the room.*

color changes everything   29

IN MY KITCHEN *breakfast nook, I added color overhead with the painted ceiling—kind of like seeing the sky above your head on a beautiful autumn day. Just a small, fabric Roman shade adds a pop of color and pulls the fall color scheme together.*

The breakfast table pays tribute to my new use of bold color. Though I always tell my customers to have a good set of basic white dishes, this modern vintage dishware collection breaks that rule and reminds me that color can instantly change a room.

THIS CRIMSON-RED LACE *fabric chair sits boldly in a side parlor at the home of Beth and Mike Fox. The hand-blown chandelier was custom-made for this room. In an otherwise neutral space, the dazzling colors placed at ceiling height make the room much more complete.*

JULIE WANTED EACH of her grown daughters to participate
in the redesign of their home in the country. I love seeing a
traditional Victorian end table repurposed with the use of bright
coral. The geometric black and white area rug anchors the bed
and gives the whole room a modern vibe. The dresser that is
shown on page 22 of this chapter sits across from the bed.

TWO OF JULIE'S *bathrooms are special for very different reasons. In the upstairs hallway guest bath, Julie used a bold coastal paint color on the walls and picked up the corals and pinks of the girls' guest rooms. When her girls return home for a visit, she sets out fresh flowers in this cone, a souvenir from her daughter's wedding, to hold the arrangement.*

I love the graphic design of this wallpaper that she used in the downstairs powder room off the kitchen. The green picks up the walls from the eat-in kitchen, and is on trend with the current use of bold wallpapers.

JULIE'S GROWN-UP DAUGHTERS *still look pretty in pink, and in this*
daughter's room the love affair with her favorite color continues.

THE ORANGE LOVE *seat in the front window of Anne and Andy's den coupled with the bright blue monogram pillow says "notice me" in a good way.*

the comfort zone

OTHING ADDS MORE comfort to a room than the smart layering of fabrics. I love to see bold geometrics mixed with traditional plaids, and I am always swayed toward black and white fabric, which makes a room look smartly tailored. One of the most affordable ways to update a room is through the use of fabric. While rugs and furniture are more expensive to change out, a great window-seat cover or a fabric drapery panel can give a room a whole new life. I like to have seasonal options in fabrics, too—such as my decision to have two sets of skirts for my dining room chairs and pillow patterns that can be switched out for summer and winter.

When reimagining your rooms, consider my new favorite option: drapery panels with contrasting trims. They add such depth to a room. For years in my living room I preferred shuttered windows. As I worked with clients to design their draperies, over time I came to appreciate how much depth and style window dressings can add to a room.

In Beth Fox's home office, I love the way the same neutral palette allows her colorful fabric to steal the show. In her building plans, she decided to place her office right inside the front door of the large stately entry to the home.

Or on a simpler scale, choose sumptuous pillows with bold geometrics, bed linens in layers that invite rest, and smart and sophisticated upholstery that encourages you to sit down and stay awhile.

Each beautiful room in this chapter will show us how fabric informed the most basic decorating decision of the room and why fabrics play such a starring role in every room's success.

"*Nothing adds more comfort to a room than the smart layering of fabrics.*"

ACROSS FROM THE *bed is a large secretary and black and white plaid wing chair. The secretary's cubbies are equipped with drinks, chocolates, and all of the niceties that out-of-town guests could wish for.*

I ADORE MARSEE'S *use of black and white damask in her guest room that she designed for her son's visits home. The print collection of wall art, with its bright green ferns, gives year-round freshness to the room. The walls are painted in the color of sweet corn, which adds warmth in winter and a sunny disposition all year. When family is not visiting, this room is the perfect guest room.*

the comfort zone   41

*"Fabric panels add depth
and style to any room."*

ACROSS FROM BETH'S *desk in her formal office is a wonderful little French étagère,
which looks so rich when paired with this oil painting. The large drapery panels that
accent her front windows bring all of the colors and formality together in one corner of
the room.*

*Beth's office fireplace, situated across from her desk, repeats the bright colors of her
fabric choice in this fireside chair. It's one of her favorite spots to relax.*

THE MASTER BEDROOM *is quite spacious and Julie was able to include a seating area at one end of the room. It provides an excellent morning spot to have coffee and read the paper. I love the tailored gray and cream houndstooth fabric with the modern wide-striped lumbar pillow. Taken all together, you can see why this well-planned and coordinated room is one that all of us at Nell Hill's love and enjoyed designing with Julie.*

UPSTAIRS IN THE *master suite, this black chest of drawers serves as a side table to the bed. The gray and yellow draperies are trimmed in a flat flange of sunny yellow linen that adds contrast to the dark furniture.*

ACROSS FROM THE *bed, Julie had her kitchen designer compose a large wall of built-ins in an effort to eliminate the need for freestanding dressers. All of their personal accessories can now be stored out of sight with the television, providing an organized retreat. The architectural gray color of the kitchen cabinets (page 25) was carried upstairs and repeated in the master suite.*

JUST BELOW THE *master bedroom, Julie's living room sits at the front of the center-hall floor plan and overlooks the large lake area of the property. The room provides multiple seating areas and showcases the perfect blend of fabrics and patterns. This room at the front door sets the color palette for the entire house, and it lets the outdoors in year-round with the open window views that are punctuated with Roman half shades.*

MARSEE'S LIVING ROOM *is the most pleasing blend of whites and neutrals. This monogrammed side chair and brasserie table anchor the space at the back of the room, right outside the sunroom door. Two chairs and a round ottoman define the fireplace seating and face away from the sunroom at their back.*

the big picture

HEN I BUILT my new store in Kansas City in 2007 I learned firsthand about planning rooms from the foundation up. Looking at a blank slate of land is far different from the experiences I have had remodeling and redesigning rooms within an existing blueprint. When I designed my new store, I wanted to be able to have many rooms within the store. It must be like what scientists feel when they're in the laboratory. I wanted to have many opportunities to be a design mixologist—and I wanted to design and redesign to my heart's content.

In my home, over the years I have frequently redesigned the seating area that sits at one end of my long living room. Here, for the first time, I recently added drapery panels to redefine the space and opted for a more modern sofa style. The fabric pattern of the draperies is subtle against my soft, buttery yellow walls and adds a warmth and texture to the room that makes me wonder how I lived without this added softness before. For my drapes, I opted for a flat flange trim with mitered corners.

One of the things I've loved about working with the customers featured in this book is the amazement I have when I see how they, too, redesigned their walls from the ground up. It is no small task to figure out where you want your rooms to be located, how large should they be, and how they will function.

In this chapter, we will go together on a homes tour to see how these stylish customers designed rooms that are both beautiful and functional. The rooms in this chapter are situated in the heart of the home and inspire the rooms in the rest of the house. Enjoy!

"This master bedroom is dressed up in some of my favorite combinations of black, whites, and creams."

THIS ROOMY MASTER *suite at Marsee's was built more than a hundred years ago, but with clever planning she was able to preserve the past qualities of the room, while modernizing the design.*

The winter-wheat walls are subtle and warm, adding depth to the large sunny suite that wraps the corner on the back of her Tudor home. Just beyond the bed, notice the bright salmon tile of the master bath. She was not swayed by pressure to tear out the fifties modern tiles, but instead she reinvented the past and claimed the small bathroom's history as part of her own new story.

the big picture   55

I LOVE THE *way the mirror over the dresser reflects the arrangement of artwork over the bed. Repeating various shades of whites for the accessories on the dresser further adds to the soft mood of Marsee's fabrics.*

In the guest bath across the hall, Marsee lights the scene with romantic candlelight.

"Make sure your mirror reflects something interesting to look at before you choose its location."

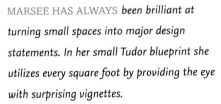

MARSEE HAS ALWAYS *been brilliant at turning small spaces into major design statements. In her small Tudor blueprint she utilizes every square foot by providing the eye with surprising vignettes.*

This nook between the dining room and kitchen will not be wasted space. Marsee made it functional and beautiful.

This small bench—a sentimental favorite—in the living room holds her collection of miniature books.

Even the tiniest powder room has power to wow. A little basket of fresh linens awaits guests.

ANNE'S GREAT ROOM *off the kitchen was cleverly situated to allow a full view of the kitchen and easy access to all of the living areas of the home.*

The sliding barn doors were reclaimed and repurposed and provide a room divider if needed. The open kitchen plan is steps away from serving in the beautiful dining room located at the front of the center-hall plan.

VIEWED FROM ANOTHER *angle, Anne's*
great room sits at the back of the house next
to the large backyard porch with fireplace. The
dark forest-green French doors define the two
spaces. The built-in cabinets were designed by
Anne and have been custom painted in a soft
bluish-green palette to give them a furniture-
finished quality. Anne changes out the mantel
seasonally to accent her color scheme—here it
is the brighter colors of autumn.

ANNE'S DINING ROOM *is grand, warm, and dramatic. I love the softness that wingback hostess chairs provide and the surprise offered by the bright geometric-patterned seats on the side chairs on either side of the buffet. The use of different chair styles adds so much interest to the room.*

THE OVERSIZED CHANDELIER—*the jewelry in this room—is so dramatic against the dark, deep color of the walls and windows.*

The centerpiece on the dining room table adds the boldness needed in this quiet room.

"By using nature's finest colors inside, this lovely home is serene and soothing."

JUST OFF THE *foyer, Anne captures more intrigue with the mood lighting of*
her small powder room. The vanity is true to Anne's use of furniture finishes
throughout the house—here she has repurposed a great cabinet and the old-
world warmth of an oversized wallpaper print.

"It's no small feat when building a home to figure out how large your rooms should be and where to locate them."

THIS COZY SEATING *area in front of the fireplace divides the room into distinct areas. Two different styles of sofas—a chesterfield style is paired with an English rolled-arm sofa—face each other and are divided by an oversized ottoman in a smartly tailored plaid fabric. One is covered in charcoal linen and the other in gray velvet.*

JULIE'S LARGE FRONT-TO-BACK *center-hall plan provides a generous blueprint for her living and dining spaces. She cleverly broke up the space with the addition of this room divider anchored by pillars. Beyond the open seating area, the formal dining room runs along the back of the home, but the open doorway allows you to see all the way to the front of the home through the living room.*

LARGE WHITE URNS *stand guard over the sideboard, repeating the pattern of the large white columns that stand at the entry to the space. The large lantern-style chandelier provides not just drama but also a central focal point for the room.*

Julie placed buffets for storage at either side of the room. I love the way both of these pieces work together but are distinctively different. The bright, sunny dining room space features the family's French country chairs and a table to match. The redesigned chairs, although diminutive in size, are elevated in stature by their stylish monograms. These family heirlooms, reupholstered in slate-gray leather, now hold their own in this large room.

SITTING NEXT TO *the dining room and across the center hall at the back of the home, Julie's kitchen echoes the color scheme of the living areas. A stylish tray holds the cook's necessities close at hand.*

SITUATED ON THE *second floor just above the living room, the master bedroom follows the same blueprint as the lower level and repeats the gray color scheme. Here a soothing oil painting over the bench sets the stage for the entrance to a gorgeous spa-like master bath. Beyond the glossy black door, the freestanding claw-foot tub is a work of art in itself.*

NEXT TO THE *tub, this glass-front cabinet is filled with all the amenities of the well-appointed retreat. I love plain white towels! They always look fresh and they go with any décor.*

The vanity, topped in white marble, sits next to the walk-in shower. The glossy black door breaks up the wall and provides a private room for the lavatory. Notice the tile pattern of the floor—how clever that the design mimics the look of an area rug.

At Nell Hill's we believe in making statements that are refined enough to be found in a dining room but surprising and elegant when added to the bathroom design, such as the floral display on the vanity.

romancing
the room

HE HOMES WE live in today serve as our sanctuaries. From cozy bedrooms to luxurious baths, homeowners are finding all kinds of ways to provide refuge and comfort in beautiful rooms. We all need that one place all to ourselves where we can go to refresh and relax. Nell Hill's style is all about surrounding ourselves with those little extras that make our spaces warm and wonderful, restful in spite of our busy lives, and always inviting to guests.

In the beautiful rooms of this book, you will find those little romantic touches like fine chocolates carefully chosen for adult children returning home, fresh bath salts and soaps arranged with soft cotton towels, and private reading nooks and cozy outdoor fireplaces decorated with as much care as any room inside. Even the well-equipped kitchen can provide refuge for the cook of the house with artfully arranged accessories and carefully chosen artwork.

Notice how Beth's formal living area was placed in the interior of the home, situated between her office and the large great room and kitchen. She announced its presence by cleverly placing seating on the back of the sofa, facing out just beyond the large arched entry. The alcoves on either side of the fireplace offer a recessed spot to add lighting and matching mirrors that give the illusion of much more depth to the room. The arched plaster walls, an architectural detail throughout the house, give the rooms a warm old-world feeling of comfort.

The sizzle of any room—the bling—is in the artful way everything is arranged. At Nell Hill's we have a tool kit of recommendations to help customers put the finishing touches on the room. In this chapter we will observe all of the things that take a room to that next level of style and romance. I like to think that just as a little black dress looks fabulous when accessorized properly, a well-designed room should have its own jewelry, too.

"Aim to always surprise and delight with the way artwork is displayed, placed, and curated in individual collections."

IF YOU ASKED *me to choose a single defining style for Nell Hill's design, it would be the way we think about the use of artwork. Good artwork is timeless and so important in the design of our space at home. Art can take your eye down a long hallway, define the stairwell with style and grace, make a cubby seem special, or tell a story. The most imaginative collections of artwork are made up of a mix of like-minded frames as well as modern styles and treatments.*

"Enlighten yourself when it comes to your lighting options—it is so impactful whether it's daytime or night."

ROMANTIC CANDLELIGHT, MATCHING *table lamps, large hurricanes, stunning chandeliers, or natural sunlight—nothing makes a room shine more than the choice of lighting. Setting the right mood in any room is so important to successful design. Whether you're illuminating a romantic table for two or just curling up in your favorite chair, controlling the lights can switch a room from great to sublime!*

"Bringing the natural world into the home is key to any room's success— think of branches and grasses as well, not just flower arrangements."

SOMETIMES I JUST *go out in my yard and choose a branch to use as an anchor in a display I'm creating inside for the season. Nothing makes me happier than to be able to use the greens or branches right outside my door and to combine them with fresh blooms of the season. I have traditionally leaned toward selecting flowers of all one color—and I usually choose whites and creamy whites. But along with the evolution of bold, bright colors in home décor, my taste for pops of pinks and all shades of greens has evolved. I am always amazed to see what inventive ways we can come up with to highlight the bounty of the season.*

*"I have fallen hard for chairs—
they should never take a backseat
to a room's success."*

I ADMIT, *I have a love affair with chairs of all shapes and sizes—and benches and window seats,*
too. I love the warm and personal look that a great chair can add to a setting or room arrangement.
Seeing great host chairs at a dining table, a seating area in a master bedroom, or a corner highlighted
with the placement of a one-of-a-kind chair—it makes my heart sing. At Nell Hill's we are also excited
about the many ways that monograms can be incorporated into the room's accessories. Meet all of
my favorite characters! If you have an heirloom chair that you have not known what to do with but
you can't part with it—maybe you'll find something here to inspire you.

"These little beauties are essential to making a home stylish, colorful, and comfortable."

I COULD NOT *live without a collection of interesting pillows in every room of the house. A day without pillows is like a day without sunshine—my mood would darken quickly. Nothing adds more pizzazz and a quicker pick-me-up in a room than a beautiful and sumptuous pillow—or three or four or five, depending on the room.*

I love the way that well-designed pillows take a master bedroom from off-limits with doors closed to "wow, check this out," or how they make a guest area seem so much more comfortable and inviting. Down-filled forms covered in yummy fabrics and trimmed in special contrasting flanges are well worth the investment in any setting. In fact, pillows can be one of the most feasible ways to upgrade your décor. And you can experiment more with pillows than you would with big upholstery pieces. One pillow added to the wing chair in the living room can turn a good chair into a great one and can give it a whole new life.

"Mirrors reflect not just light but also good taste."

IT IS SO *interesting to see the room through reflective glass. Make sure there is something interesting to look at when hanging a mirror. Start by holding up the mirror where you think you want it placed, and see what reflects across the room. I love the way a mirror can add light and sparkle to an area—over a bar, in a tight corner, and above vanities in the bathrooms of the home. When deciding on your bathroom mirrors, consider adding a real surprise there, especially in powder rooms. Adding glass accessories to the same area—apothecary jars, glass canisters, bowls, vases, gazing balls, and a well-placed table lamp—will make the whole scene sparkle. Tuck in a few pieces of silver and you can build a dramatic tableau that will sparkle and elevate the room instantly.*

"I am a bit obsessed with trays and platters—they are the perfect foil for all kinds of collections and tableaus."

PLATTERS HUNG ON *walls, trays lined up against kitchen counters and holding everyday utensils, or even one outside atop urns. . . . Give me one beautiful tray and I will figure out how to use it. I love trays inside and outside. I love them for serving and I love them as collections. At Nell Hill's we somewhat pride ourselves on figuring out inventive ways to use trays. If you fall in love with a tray—take it home. You will find a clever way to use it as these homeowners have in this book. On large ottomans, stack your favorite books. Next to the range, assemble your favorite cooking accessories. On a dresser, create a fantastic collection of your favorite photos. In the guest bath, add candles and scented soaps. Use your imagination—a good tray always carries its creative weight!*

"The largest space of our homes is often right outside our doors. Make your green space work overtime for you. Or bring your green space inside to create a natural environment."

OVER THE YEARS, Nell Hill's has gained a bit of fame for the way we use garden statuary and urns in our decorating. For a while now, I have been known to set my formal dining table with large metal and concrete pieces, never shying away from bringing a great garden piece indoors. (I hide protective plastic under the table runners.) Or for the spaces on my porch and garden, when I am hosting an event outdoors, it is likely you will find a garden urn doing double duty as a serving piece. I love to layer trays and mirrors outside on my urns where guests can find a cold drink waiting or a few appetizers set out. The only rule you will find when it comes to bringing the outdoors in and the indoors out is that you must use your imagination (and be careful lifting)!

Marsee is also a master of bringing the outdoors in. Look at how she has used garden statuary throughout her house to remind us that nature inspires all of our decorating. In the dining room, a large garden cherub and black metal urn bring focus to the center of the room and drama dresses her dining room table throughout the year.

country home

country estate

DESIGN PORTFOLIO

Beth and Mike Fox

english tudor cottage

DESIGN PORTFOLIO

Marsee and Mike Bates

suburban rebuild

DESIGN PORTFOLIO

Anne and Andy Epstein

greek revival

acknowledgments

I WANT TO THANK those generous homeowners who graciously welcomed me into their homes and shared their personal style and grace with me. A special thanks, from the bottom of my heart, goes out to Julie and Marc Wenger, Anne and Andy Epstein, Marsee and Mike Bates, and Beth and Mike Fox. They so generously shared their time with us, and I am so grateful for their contributions to this book and their support.

A special thank you, too, to two people who put their creative talents and experience together to make this book possible—editorial director Jean Lowe and photographer Bob Greenspan.

Thank you to the publishing team at Andrews McMeel Publishing for their continued support of my book program—editor Dorothy O'Brien, production editor Christi Clemons Hoffman, and the talented designers Julie Barnes, for a beautiful jacket, and Diane Marsh, who designed the interior pages.

None of this would be possible without my dedicated, faithful store employees and friends, whose contributions to making Nell Hill's successful are immeasurable. I am so grateful to them for their help and talent.

I am blessed with dear friends who are always there for me.

And, always, my heart is with my dear customers who continually teach me about their style, who generously share their lives with me, and who always show up—I am especially grateful for your support.

Finally, I want to acknowledge the Global Orphan Project, a charitable organization that is near and dear to my heart. This organizaiton provides the development of living environments, education, and support for children living in underdeveloped and impoverished countries, who might otherwise not have a future available to them. I am grateful to Mike and Beth Fox for introducing me to this project. You make the world a better place!